LIFE IN THE FAST LANE

ON A
JET SKI

H. PHILLIPS

Published in 2015 by Cavendish Square Publishing, LLC
243 5th Avenue, Suite 136, New York, NY 10016

Copyright © 2015 by Cavendish Square Publishing, LLC

First Edition

This publication represents the opinions and views of the author based on his or her personal
experience, knowledge, and research. The information in this book serves as a general guide
only. The author and publisher have used their best efforts in preparing this book and disclaim
liability rising directly or indirectly from the use and application of this book.

CPSIA Compliance Information: Batch #WS14CSQ

All websites were available and accurate when this book was sent to press.

Library of Congress Cataloging-in-Publication Data
Phillips, H.
On a jet ski / by H. Phillips.
p. cm. — (Life in the fast lane)
Includes index.
ISBN 978-1-62713-046-2 (hardcover) ISBN 978-1-62713-048-6 (ebook)
1. Jet skiing — Juvenile literature. I. Phillips, H. II. Title.
GV840.J4 P45 2015
797.3—d23

Editorial Director: Dean Miller
Art Director: Jeffrey Talbot
Production Manager: Jennifer Ryder-Talbot
Production Editor: David McNamara

Packaged for Cavendish Square Publishing, LLC by BlueApple*Works* Inc.
Managing Editor: Melissa McClellan
Designer: Tibor Choleva
Photo Research: Joshua Avramson, Melissa McClellan
Copy Editor: Janis Dyer

CONTENTS

Jet skiing is a high-powered water sport.

INTRODUCTION

The feeling of freedom when riding a jet ski is like no other. You can hardly see from the wind and the water hitting your face. At this speed, things go by very quickly. You bound over waves and swells, keeping an eye out for other boats and crafts. Wave to your friends watching from shore!

A jet ski is high-powered, fast excitement on the water. The first jet ski was released over forty years ago, and they have been growing in popularity ever since. Each year, more and more people cruise and skim the waters of their local rivers, lakes, and oceans on this **personal watercraft**.

If you like the water and the beach, then you might want to explore the sport of jet skiing. A jet ski lets you drive yourself at high speeds over water. Jet skis are fun and exciting. But jet skiing is not a sport for reckless daredevils. It's a sport that people of all ages can enjoy. Jet skiing can be as safe as it is thrilling.

Standing on a jet ski is similar to waterskiing.

THE INVENTION OF THE JET SKI

You may have heard of a Jet Ski and wondered what it was. When people talk about jet skis, they mean personal watercrafts (PWC)—Jet Ski is just one type, like a Ford is a type of car. People today use PWCs for water fun and competition—unlike larger boats that transport people and things or can be fishing vessels. Today people call all types of PWCs Jet Skis, not just the one brand.

An inventor named Clayton Jacobsen II built the first jet ski in the early 1960s. He designed the first jet ski in his home in Arizona. Jacobson enjoyed dirt bike racing, but he wanted to avoid crashes on the hard ground. He decided to build a self-powered water ski that he could use on the lakes of his home state of Arizona.

Jacobsen's first jet ski was a cross between a motorcycle, a speedboat, and a jet aircraft. Like a motorcycle, Jacobsen's jet ski was steered using handlebars. Like a motorboat, it was made to travel very quickly across water. Finally, the jet ski was powered by a unique system of jet propulsion.

A New Kind of Engine

Most boats are powered by **propellers**, but jet skis could not be used safely if they had propellers. If the rider were to fall off, the propeller could cause serious injury as it continued to spin. Jacobsen understood this problem when he built the first jet ski. He needed to invent a different kind of propulsion system. He finally decided that jet propulsion would do as good a job as a propeller—and jet propulsion would be safer for the rider.

Jacobsen used an **impeller** to power his jet ski. An impeller is a type of propeller that has been fitted into a tunnel. The engine spins the impeller, which pulls water from the front of the jet ski. The impeller pressurizes the water inside the tunnel. When enough pressure is built up, the water shoots out of the tunnel through a nozzle at the rear of the craft. As the impeller continues to spin, the pressurized water continues to shoot out the back of

**Pressurized water shoots out
of the nozzle at the rear of jet skis.**

Drivers use a **throttle** to control the jet ski's speed.

ON A JET SKI

the jet ski. The pressurized water is what moves the jet ski, not the impeller! Now the jet ski can be driven like any other boat.

The Original Jet Ski

The public saw Jacobsen's first jet ski in the mid-1960s. A company named Bombardier bought Jacobsen's invention and tried to sell it. They were not successful. Boating was just becoming popular for most people. A single-person watercraft was not useful for families. People wanted to be on boats in groups, not riding around one at a time.

In the early 1970s, Kawasaki bought the invention from Bombardier and introduced the Jet Ski watercraft. People were now

FAST FACTS

Jet skis have become very popular for several reasons. Jet skis are comfortable, stable, and easy to use. They can be enjoyed on all types of waterways, including lakes, rivers, and oceans. Jet skis are a fun and exciting way to spend time with friends and family.

used to boating. They owned boats that could carry several people. Now they wanted one that could be used for sport fun. Kawasaki was able to sell its jet ski. It became so successful that jet skis soon were seen on rivers, lakes, and oceans around the world.

Originally, Jacobsen invented two types of jet skis. Both were powered by jet propulsion. The difference was that a rider sat on one and stood on the other.

Kawasaki's first jet ski only allowed riders to stand. This jet ski was a platform with a long handlebar. To steer, the driver had to lean to one side or another. This jet ski really acted like a ski!

Jet Skis Today

As time passed, many people found that riding while sitting was better. In the 1980s, companies began to develop PWCs that could seat two and three riders. These jet skis were more stable and safer for riders. In the 1990s, companies continued to improve the design of jet skis to make them easier to use and more comfortable. Today, many PWCs can carry three passengers and reach speeds of 60 miles per hour (over 95 km/h). There are competitions around the United States for both stand-up and sit-down jet skis. Popular manufacturers of PWCs are Yamaha, Kawasaki, Sea-Doo, and Honda.

Stand up PWC

Sit down PWC, with two seats

These riders are competing in a jet ski slalom race.

2 LET THE RACE BEGIN!

Both stand-up and sit-down PWCs can be used for a relaxing ride on lakes, rivers, and oceans, but many people like to race them as well. Competing with friends and family on the water can be a great way to have fun and get some outdoor exercise. Plus, the feeling you get from winning a race can't be beat! It doesn't matter what type of PWC people own— they can use them in a variety of different types of races.

There are four different types of racing that are popular for PWCs. These are **slalom**, **freestyle**, **endurance**, and **drag racing**. Many different riders choose the race they participate in based on the type of racing they like. Endurance racing, for example, makes for a very long race, but is also relatively safe, with little chance of colliding into another driver. Drag racing is the easiest kind of racing, and is all about speed. Drag racers go in a straight line and attempt to go as far and fast as possible.

Today, over 200 clubs in more than fifty countries around the world promote jet watercraft racing. Races are organized into local, national, and international events. Local events are for anyone who wants to try racing. Over 43 national championships are held worldwide to choose the best racers who will participate in the world finals. The world finals are held each year in Arizona. Over 750 of world's best racers participate in this event.

Zigzags

The most popular style of jet ski racing is the slalom event. The slalom event is held on a zigzag course. Riders start the race near the shore. When the flag drops, they race forward and weave in and out through floating markers. These **buoys** mark the slalom course over the water. The slalom race has two runs. There is a one-minute rest between each race. The rider with the fastest time for both races wins.

In an official slalom race, the course is 283 feet (80 m) long and is lined with nine buoys. At each buoy, the riders have to make a turn of some kind. The direction in

Women excel at jet ski racing.

Freestyle jet ski racers can perform amazing tricks.

which the riders must turn depends on the color of the buoy. A red buoy means turn left. A yellow buoy means turn right. Sometimes the turns are very sharp. Being able to **maneuver** these turns with speed and accuracy is the most important thing for racers.

Tricks and Freestyle

Another major style of PWC racing is the freestyle competition. The freestyle event is not so much a race as it is a ballet on the water. In freestyle competitions, riders show their skill in performing creative tricks and difficult maneuvers. Each competitor gets two minutes to put together the best possible combination of tricks. The rider is then given a score between one and ten. One is the lowest score and ten is the highest. In an official freestyle competition, there are always seven judges. Each judge gives a score to a rider. These scores are then added up and divided by seven to get the average score. The highest final score wins the competition.

There are dozens of different tricks one can do on a jet watercraft. Freestyle riders come up with new tricks all the time.

Here are six popular jet ski tricks:

1 **The Tail Stand**
   This is a good trick for beginners.
   A rider must have good balance for this
   trick. The driver pulls the nose (**bow**) of
   the jet ski into the air and holds it there
   as long as he or she can. Pulling a tail
   stand is a lot like popping a wheelie
   on a bike.

2 **The Barrel Roll**
   This trick is easy and a lot of fun. When
   a rider does a barrel roll, she rolls the jet
   ski over and dunks herself in the water.
   It's important that the rider doesn't let go
   when she is underwater, or the jet ski will
   be stuck upside-down.

3 **Barefooting**
   This trick requires a rider to take both
   her feet off the ski. She swings one leg
   over so it is beside the other, and then
   she steps off, while the ski is still moving.
   Doing this trick while moving takes a lot
   of time and practice. Barefooting also
   takes courage! Experienced barefoot
   riders can throw up an awesome spray
   of water.

This rider is performing a tail stand.

4 The Hurricane

This trick looks great, but it is very diffi-cult. The hurricane takes twice the skill of doing a tail stand or a barrel roll. To do this trick right, a rider spins the jet water-craft around in tight circles. The challeng-ing part of this trick is that the rider must take his foot off the ski. Only the most ex-perienced riders should try the hurricane.

5 The Fountain

The fountain is a display trick. A rider shifts her balance toward the front of the watercraft while it is in motion. For

Jet ski riders getting ready to perform the hurricane trick.

a moment the nose may go underwater. This move kicks up the rear end (**stern**) and makes the jet ski shoot water into the air. The rider has turned her jet ski into a water fountain!

6 The Turning Sub
To do the turning sub, a rider needs a lot of weight or strength. If the rider isn't heavy, he or she can learn to use the force of the jet ski to do this trick. While moving, the rider must push the jet ski all the way under the water. First the nose will go underwater. The rider follows.

Once under water, the rider has to be able to turn the jet ski. The end result is that the watercraft comes out from under the water going in a different direction than when it went under. Professional freestyle riders can make this trick look easy even though it is not.

Seeing top PWC riders perform these and other tricks is thrilling for audiences everywhere. For many families, travelling to the beach to watch PWC competitions is a enjoyable way to spend the day. They bring a picnic and spread themselves out on the sand, cheering for their favorites and hoping to see an exciting new trick or closely contested race.

FAST FACTS

The 2013 IJSBA (International Jet Sports Boating Assn.) World Finals took place in October, 2013, in Arizona. It focused on **closed-course** racing and freestyle competition. Men and women from over fifty countries participated. The top five countries were the United States, Thailand, Norway, Kuwait, and Canada.

Jet ski racers at the beginning of a slalom race.

The whole family can have fun jet skiing.

3 JET SKI EQUIPMENT

People of all ages and abilities can enjoy jet skiing. It is an exciting and thrilling way to spend a day, and a great way to get out in the sun. You don't need to buy a jet ski to try it—you can rent one at first.

The experience of jet skiing is a unique feeling. It is much like riding a motorcycle, but less dangerous because jet skiing is done on water. Falling off a motorcycle can be deadly. Falling off a jet ski is less risky. Water cushions the fall, so jet ski riders don't need to worry as much about injury.

Falling from a jet ski can be frightening, however. You need to always be aware that you could fall off a jet ski. As long as you follow basic safety rules, you will be safe.

The average jet watercrafts only run up to 45 miles per hour (72 km/h). Forty-five miles per hour on the water feels a lot faster than it does on the highway. It feels that way because you are so close to the water.

Jet skis used in competition can run up to 70 miles per hour (112 km/h). Competition jet skis are not toys. Operating a racing jet ski is dangerous and should be left to the pros.

Use The Proper Equipment

To fully enjoy jet skiing, a rider needs to stay safe. The best way to stay safe is to know your watercraft and the equipment needed to ride it. The jet ski is not the only piece of watercraft equipment about which you need to know.

FAST FACTS

The **lanyard** is a very useful tool when jet skiing. This small cord connects to one end of the on/off switch on the jet ski and the other end is tied around the rider's wrist. If a rider falls off the jet ski, the lanyard is pulled out and the engine is shut off. This is important because if the motor kept running, the jet ski would drive away by itself, leaving the rider stranded in the middle of the lake—or the ocean!

Jet skiers love the thrill of going fast.

The most important piece of equipment is a life jacket. A life jacket is a personal flotation device (PFD). A PFD is worn like a vest. It is made of foam rubber and is brightly colored to attract attention. A PFD is designed to keep a person's head above water after a fall. This is important for any water sport because a PFD keeps a person safe even if he or she is knocked unconscious in an accident.

Riders must wear their life jackets when jet skiing.

A rider must wear a PFD while riding any kind of personal watercraft. This is the law. Anyone who jet skis without a PFD is running the risk of arrest as well as the risk of injury. You should also attach a whistle to your PFD in case you need to call for help.

Other recommended pieces of equipment are wet suits, gloves, eye protection, and footwear. None of these are required, but using them helps riders in many ways.

All riders should wear safety gear such as helmets and goggles.

Wet suits are made to keep you warm. If you plan on using a jet ski in the northern United States, the water will be cold until the hottest part of summer. A wet suit lets you stay in the water for hours. Gloves protect your hands from blisters. Footwear, such as rubber surf shoes, protects your feet from sharp rocks while you get your jet ski in and out of the water.

After your PFD, protecting your eyes is the next most important safety tip. It's awfully hard to see and control your PWC if you get hit in the eye while speeding along the water. Some people use sunglasses, but you're better off with goggles.

FAST FACTS

You may be riding in the cool water, but your jet ski engine can still overheat. If you find that the base of your watercraft is too hot to touch, you should turn the motor off and take a break. An overworked jet ski engine can actually catch on fire. You should also check if your PWC has a portable fire extinguisher for an emergency.

There are many places that rent jet skis.

4 STAYING SAFE

Even though jet skis can be a lot of fun, you have to pay close attention when you are riding one. They may be small and fun to use, but the U.S. Coast Guard considers all jet watercraft Class A boats, and they hold the driver responsible for anything that happens with the PWC. So being smart, safe, and avoiding accidents are top priorities when using your PWC.

Staying safe while jet skiing involves following the rules and using your head. You need to follow important rules and regulations to be safe while using a jet watercraft. First, you must have a valid boating license or certificate. To get this certificate, most states require you to take a boating safety course. You also need to have a valid driver's license and be at least sixteen years old to drive a jet ski.

Make sure to read the jet ski's owner's manual before you try it. You need to understand your PWC's features and controls.

It is also helpful to take at least one lesson on how to use a jet ski safely before trying it on your own. In addition, it is important to register your PWC before you take it on the water. When a watercraft is registered, it receives an identification number. Identification numbers are just like license

plate numbers. They are used in case of an accident or if someone is driving recklessly.

Using the right equipment is another way to stay safe. Make sure to wear a U.S. Coast Guard-approved PFD that fits properly. Life jackets save lives, and wearing one is the most important rule in riding a PWC.

Lifeguards use jet skis to rescue swimmers.

You should also attach a whistle to your life jacket in case you need to signal for help. Many areas also require that you wear a helmet while riding a jet ski.

Do not use alcohol or drugs while driving a jet watercraft of any kind. The penalty for breaking this law is the same as for a person driving a car while **intoxicated**. The influence of drugs and alcohol makes the sport of jet skiing deadly. You endanger yourself along with everyone else on the water if you drive while intoxicated. The U.S. Coast Guard's advice is, "Be a sober skipper." Follow this advice so that everyone on the water can have fun.

FAST FACT

To stay safe while riding a jet ski, there are things you shouldn't do. For example, don't weave in and out between other boats on the water. Don't try tricks and jumps before you're ready. Don't go near areas where people are swimming or fishing, and stay away from wildlife. Don't use your jet ski at night. Finally, don't spin around or quickly change directions without carefully checking for other watercraft.

Maintaining balance while jet skiing takes strength and a lot of skill.

Going fast is not allowed in "No Wake" zones.

Finally, another important way to stay safe is to be aware of local restrictions. A lot of waterways in the United States do not allow PWCs. There are even more areas that have speed limits. The most common restriction you will find is "No Wake." The **wake** is the waves created behind a boat as it moves in the water. A "No Wake" zone means that all boats must go slowly because their wake could be damaging to the shore or to other boats.

ON A JET SKI

Now that you know about jet skis, look for races and competitions in your area to attend or even watch videos online. Starting out as a spectator is great and it may inspire you to get out there and enter the next competition. No matter why you want to ride a jet ski—the thrill of the race, the excitement of tricks, or just to hang out at the beach with family and friends, the most important rule is to have fun.

FAST FACTS

When you are riding a jet ski, you must remember that you are sharing the water with other boats. Any boat larger than a jet ski gets the right of way, meaning it gets priority in the water. The reason is simple—the larger the boat, the longer it takes to turn. Safe boating means staying away from other boats.

WORDS TO KNOW

bow: the front of a boat or watercraft

buoy: a plastic ball or cone that is tied to the bottom of the lake and marks a slalom course

closed-course: a competition in which riders ride laps of a course

drag racing: a competition in which riders compete on a short course at top speed

endurance: a competition that takes place over long distances

freestyle: a competition in which riders do as many tricks as possible in a limited amount of time

impeller: a propeller that is set inside the body of a watercraft

intoxicated: when a person uses alcohol or drugs and loses control of their behavior

lanyard: a safety cord tied to the jet ski's on/off button and the driver's wrist

maneuver: a series of movements that require skill

personal watercraft: any sort of small boat, such as a jet ski, that is meant for recreation and is ridden by one or two people

propeller: a device with two or more blades that turn quickly to push a boat forward

slalom: a form of racing for jet watercraft that involves riding in a zigzag pattern through a buoyed race course

stern: the back of a boat or watercraft

throttle: the device that a driver uses to control the power of the engine

wake: the waves created behind a boat as it moves through the water

FURTHER READING

Books

Boats (Mean Machines)
Mark Morris
Hampshire, UK
Raintree
2004

Personal Watercraft
E.S. Budd
North Mankato, MN
Child's World Incorporated
2012

RYA Personal Watercraft Handbook
Peter Gavin, Candice Abbott
Southampton, UK
Royal Yachting Association
2011

Websites

Boat Smart Canada
www.boatsmartcanada.com
This website tells you all about how to get
a Pleasure Craft Operating Card, important
rules about watercraft safety, and even lets
you take the boating license exam online.

Discover Boating
www.discoverboating.com
Discover Boating is a website devoted to
all sorts of recreational watercraft, and they
have lots of information about the require-
ments for riding a PWC.

Personal Watercraft
www.personalwatercraft.com
This site features articles, reviews,
and videos about all types of
personal watercraft.

RESOURCES

Organizations

International Jet Sports
Boating Association (IJSBA)
Half Moon Bay, CA
Phone: (714) 751-8695
www.ijsba.com
This is the official site of the International
Jet Sports Boating Association. Check out
this site to learn about event schedules,
race results, and competitors. You'll also
find the IJSBA official competition rulebook.

Personal Watercraft Industry Association
(PWIAC)
Washington, DC
Phone: (202) 737-9763
www.pwia.org
This organization promotes the
safe and responsible operation
of personal watercraft.

INDEX

About the Author

H. Phillips is a racing enthusiast who lives in Indiana, where he has attended the famed Indy 500 for years. A native of upstate New York, H. spent his teenage years racing dirt bikes through back roads.